# Overseas Voting: The Uniformed and Overseas Citizens Absentee Voting Act

Robert Timothy Reagan

Federal Judicial Center

2016

This Federal Judicial Center publication was undertaken in furtherance of the Center's statutory mission to develop and conduct research and education programs for the judicial branch. While the Center regards the content as responsible and valuable, it does not reflect policy or recommendations of the Board of the Federal Judicial Center.

FIRST PRINTING

# Contents

Introduction  1
History  1
Remedies  3
Forty-Five Days  7
Federal Write-In Absentee Ballot  15
Territories  17
Standing  16
Equal Protection  22
Privacy  23
State Elections  25
Conclusion  26
Appendix:  The Uniformed and Overseas Citizens Absentee Voting Act  27

# Introduction

The Uniformed and Overseas Citizens Absentee Voting Act (UOCAVA) requires the federal and state governments to facilitate overseas citizens' participation in federal elections. This includes enabling overseas citizens to register and vote. In particular, jurisdictions must be able to send out absentee ballots to overseas voters at least forty-five days before federal elections.

The enfranchisement of overseas voters began with military personnel, extended to their families, and then extended to citizens who are overseas for other reasons. An overseas citizen is typically eligible to vote in the last location of a stateside domicile.

# History

"Immediately prior to the Civil War, only one state—Pennsylvania—had provisions that permitted absent servicemen to vote, but by 1864 nineteen of twenty-five Union states, and seven of eleven Confederate states, had implemented some means of allowing their soldiers to vote away from their home polling place."[1]

On September 16, 1942, President Roosevelt signed a federal act entitling members of the military serving in times of war to vote absentee in federal elections.[2] The act was amended in 1944 to provide states with recommendations on how they could facilitate absentee voting by persons away at war.[3] The amendments established a United States War Ballot Commission consisting of the Secretary of War, the Secretary of the Navy,

---

1. Steven F. Huefner, Lessons from Improvements in Military and Overseas Voting, 47 U. Rich. L. Rev. 833, 837 (2013) (footnotes omitted); *see* Alexander Keyssar, The Right to Vote 104 (2000) ("In so doing, they established a precedent for loosening the links between residence and participation in elections.").

2. Pub. L. 77-712, 56 Stat. 753 (Sept. 16, 1942); *see* Huefner, *supra* note 1, at 839–40.

3. Pub. L. 78-277, 58 Stat. 136 (Apr. 1, 1944); *see* Huefner, *supra* note 1, at 840.

and the Administrator of the War Shipping Administration.[4] The recommendations were revised in 1946.[5] The provisions of these 1940s enactments were codified in title 50 of the United States Code, concerning war, beginning with section 301.[6]

President Eisenhower signed the Federal Voting Assistance Act of 1955 on August 9 of that year, which again revised the recommendations to states for providing absentee voting to persons in the military.[7] The focus of the recommendations expanded from persons serving in the military to include civilian government employees serving overseas.[8] The revised recommendations were codified in title 42, chapter 20, concerning the elective franchise, beginning with section 1973cc.[9]

The Overseas Citizens Voting Rights Act of 1975, signed by President Ford on January 2, 1976, granted overseas citizens the right to vote in federal elections.[10] The provisions of this act were codified beginning with section 1973dd of title 42.[11]

The previous enactments were replaced by the Uniformed and Overseas Citizens Absentee Voting Act (UOCAVA), signed by President Reagan on August 28, 1986,[12] codified in title 42 of the United States Code beginning with section 1973ff.[13]

The Military and Overseas Voter Empowerment Act (MOVE Act) was subtitle I.H of the National Defense Authorization Act for Fiscal Year 2010, which was signed by President Obama on October 28, 2009.[14] Its amendments to UOCAVA included a requirement that absentee ballots in federal

---

4. Pub. L. 78-277, § 301(a), 58 Stat. at 140.

5. Pub. L. 79-348, 60 Stat. 96 (Apr. 19, 1946).

6. 50 U.S.C. §§ 301–355 (1952).

7. Pub. L. 84-296, 69 Stat. 584 (Aug. 9, 1955); *see* Huefner, *supra* note 1, at 841; Bush v. Hillsborough Cnty. Canvassing Bd., 123 F. Supp. 2d 1305, 1307–08 (N.D. Fla. 2000).

8. Pub. L. 84-296, § 101, 69 Stat. at 584; 42 U.S.C. § 1973cc (1982).

9. 42 U.S.C. §§ 1973cc to 1973cc-26 (1982).

10. Pub. L. 94-203, 89 Stat. 1142 (Jan. 2, 1976); *see* Huefner, *supra* note 1, at 841; *Bush*, 123 F. Supp. 2d at 1308–09.

11. 42 U.S.C. §§ 1973dd to 1973dd-6 (1982).

12. Pub. L. 99-410, 100 Stat. 924 (Aug. 28, 1986); *see* Huefner, *supra* note 1, at 842–43; *Bush*, 123 F. Supp. 2d at 1310–12.

13. 42 U.S.C. §§ 1973ff to 1973ff-7 (1988).

14. Pub. L. 111-84, 123 Stat. 2190, 2318–35 (2009).

elections be sent to overseas voters at least forty-five days before election day.[15] It also modernized provisions on transmission of ballot materials to include electronic transmission.[16]

In September 2014, sections of the U.S. Code pertaining to voting and elections were moved to a new title 52. UOCAVA occupies sections 20301 to 20311.

# Remedies

Common remedies for late transmittals of overseas ballots include an extension of time for their return and provisions for express delivery, including fax and email. Judges often also order notice of remedies to overseas voters.

If ballots have to be sent out before the final candidates are known, such as when a recall election is scheduled too soon after the first election, judges may order the use of blank absentee ballots or instant-runoff ballots, on which voters rank order their choices. Sometimes, judges have adjusted election dates.

If a ballot changes after absentee ballots have already been sent out, judges are sometimes called upon to specify how original ballots will be counted.

## Approving a Compressed Special Election

*Chicago Board of Election Commissioners v. Illinois State Board of Elections (Samuel Der-Yeghiayan, N.D. Ill. 1:09-cv-82)*

On January 15, 2009, U.S. District Judge Samuel Der-Yeghiayan, Northern District of Illinois, approved a proposed special election schedule to fill the U.S. House of Representatives seat that became vacant when Rahm Emanuel became President Obama's chief of staff.[17]

---

15. *Id.* § 579(a)(1)(C), 123 Stat. at 2322; UOCAVA § 102(a)(8)(A), 52 U.S.C. § 20302(a)(8)(A) (2014); *see* Huefner, *supra* note 1, at 845.

16. Pub. L. 111-84, § 577, 123 Stat. at 2319–20, UOCAVA §§ 102(a)(6), 102(e), 52 U.S.C. §§ 20302(a)(6), 20302(e); *see* Huefner, *supra* note 1, at 845.

17. Order, Chi. Bd. of Election Comm'rs v. Ill. State Bd. of Elections, No. 1:09-cv-82 (N.D. Ill. Jan. 15, 2009), D.E. 16 [hereinafter *Chi. Bd. of Election Comm'rs* Order].

On January 7, Chicago's election officials filed a federal complaint against the state board of elections to obtain the court's blessing for a time schedule to elect Emanuel's replacement that, among other things, compressed the voting time for overseas voters.[18] The special election was set for April 7 to correspond with an already-scheduled local election, with a primary set for March 3 if necessary.[19]

"Under the schedule presented by the Plaintiffs, the certification of candidate names to the March 3, 2009 special primary occurs only 36 days before the date of the Primary. There are only 35 days between the March 3, 2009 special primary and the April 7, 2009 special election."[20] Judge Der-Yeghiayan approved the use of modified blank absentee ballots that listed all candidates who filed nomination papers, email and fax transmittal of overseas ballots, and a program of notice to overseas voters.[21]

## Ordered Departures from Statutory Deadlines

*DuPage County Board of Election Commissioners v. Illinois State Board of Elections (Ruben Castillo, N.D. Ill. 1:08-cv-232)*

U.S. District Judge Ruben Castillo, Northern District of Illinois, issued an order on January 18, 2008, specifying a calendar of time requirements for a special election to fill a vacancy in the U.S. House of Representatives, including departures from normal statutory deadlines, to accommodate scheduled election dates.[22]

Election officials for seven northern Illinois counties and the City of Aurora had filed a federal complaint on January 10 seeking relief from time requirements for the special election to fill a vacancy created by the resignation of Dennis Hastert.[23] They claimed that a March 8 election with a

---

18. Complaint, *id.* (Jan. 7, 2009), D.E. 1.
19. *See id.* at 1; *see* Dan Mihalopoulos, *26 File for Emanuel's Congressional Seat*, Chi. Trib., Jan. 20, 2009, at 12 (reporting that primary elections would be held because party nominations were contested).
20. *Chi. Bd. of Election Comm'rs Order*, *supra* note 17, at 14.
21. *Id.* at 15–20.
22. Order, DuPage Cnty. Bd. of Election Comm'rs v. Ill. State Bd. of Elections, No. 1:08-cv-232 (Jan. 18, 2008), D.E. 32 [hereinafter *DuPage Cnty. Bd. of Election Comm'rs* Order].
23. Complaint, *id.* (Jan. 10, 2008), D.E. 1.

February 5 primary—the day of Illinois's Super Tuesday presidential primary—did not give the election officials enough time to comply with various state time requirements or UOCAVA.[24] The federal government sought permission to participate in the case as an amicus curiae to protect the federal rights of overseas voters.[25]

With respect to overseas ballots, Judge Castillo ordered that they be counted for the primary election if postmarked by February 4 and received by February 8.[26] Overseas ballots for the March 8 election would be accepted if postmarked by March 7 and received by March 29.[27] An important difficulty in providing overseas voters with timely ballots was the short time between the two elections, so Judge Castillo authorized the use of blank absentee ballots.[28]

## Late Absentee Ballots in Georgia

*United States v. Georgia (Charles A. Pannell, Jr., N.D. Ga. 1:04-cv-2040)*

U.S. District Judge Charles A. Pannell, Jr., Northern District of Georgia, issued written orders on July 15, 2004, providing the following relief for overseas voters: (1) Georgia will accept faxed ballots, (2) Georgia will accept Internet-based write-in absentee ballots, (3) Georgia will pay for express delivery of absentee ballots, and (4) absentee ballots will be accepted until three days after the election if mailed by election day.[29]

The Justice Department had filed a federal complaint on July 13 claiming that several counties had failed to mail overseas voters their absentee ballots in time to be returned by the day of July 20 primary elections, and the planned runoff date of August 10 did not allow for enough time to mail

---

24. *Id.*
25. Amicus Curiae Motion, *id.* (Jan. 14, 2008), D.E. 10.
26. *DuPage Cnty. Bd. of Election Comm'rs* Order, *supra* note 22, at 17.
27. *Id.* at 18.
28. *Id.* at 18–20.
29. Order, United States v. Georgia, No. 1:04-cv-2040 (N.D. Ga. July 16, 2004), D.E. 4; Order, Larios v. Cox, No. 1:03-cv-693 (N.D. Ga. July 16, 2004), D.E. 261; *see* United States v. Georgia, 892 F. Supp. 2d 1367 (N.D. Ga. 2012) (providing similar injunctive relief eight years later).

overseas voters absentee ballots.[30] On the same day, Georgia's secretary of state filed a motion seeking similar relief in a 2003 case that resulted in court-ordered redistricting for Georgia's legislature.[31] Judge Pannell, who had been assigned the 2003 case, agreed to grant immediate injunctive relief.[32]

## Improper Counting of Military Absentee Ballots in a Local Election
*Casarez v. Val Verde County (Fred Biery, W.D. Tex. 96-cv-108)*

In an action alleging dilution of Hispanic votes by local election officials' accepting military absentee ballots in a local election from voters who no longer resided in the county, U.S. District Judge Fred Biery, Western District of Texas, issued a preliminary injunction against certification of the election, finding a substantial likelihood that the ballots in question should not have been counted.[33]

Judge Biery issued the January 24, 1997, preliminary injunction in a case filed on December 19, 1996, concerning disputed results of the November 5, 1996, election of Val Verde County sheriff and one of the county's commissioners.[34]

---

30. Complaint, *United States v. Georgia*, No. 1:04-cv-2040 (N.D. Ga. July 13, 2004), D.E. 1; Motion, *id.* (July 13, 2004), D.E. 2 (seeking a temporary restraining order and a preliminary injunction).

31. Motion, *Larios*, No. 1:03-cv-693 (N.D. Ga. July 13, 2004), D.E. 259; *see* Larios v. Cox, 314 F. Supp. 2d 1357 (N.D. Ga. 2004) (approving a special master's plan); Larios v. Cox, 300 F. Supp. 2d 1320 (N.D. Ga.) (determining that legislative districts violated the principle of one person one vote), *summarily aff'd*, 542 U.S. 947 (2004).

32. Minutes, *United States v. Georgia*, No. 1:04-cv-2040 (N.D. Ga. July 14, 2004), D.E. 3; Minutes, *Larios*, No. 1:03-cv-693 (N.D. Ga. July 14, 2004), D.E. 260.

33. Casarez v. Val Verde County, 957 F. Supp. 847 (W.D. Tex. 1997); *see* Casarez v. Val Verde County, No. 2:96-cv-108, 1997 WL 258610 (W.D. Tex. May 9, 1997) (declining to dissolve the preliminary injunction in light of subsequent state court activity).

34. *Casarez*, 957 F. Supp. at 850; Docket Sheet, Casarez v. Val Verde County, No. 2:96-cv-108 (W.D. Tex. Dec. 19, 1996); *see id.* (D.E. 10, temporary restraining order issued December 20, 1996, by Judge H.F. Garcia); *Casarez*, 957 F. Supp. at 850 (noting same).

Following state court proceedings in which challenges to the validity of the votes in question were not proved, Judge Biery dissolved the preliminary injunction five months after issuing it.[35] In 1998, Judge Biery granted the defendants summary judgment.[36] He awarded the defendants costs but not attorney fees and awarded as damages salary of office for the duration of the preliminary injunction.[37]

## Forty-Five Days

Election officials must be in a position to send absentee ballots to overseas voters forty-five days in advance of a federal election. This means that it is generally not proper to hold a runoff election fewer than forty-five days after a first election. This also means that ballots should be final in advance of the forty-five-day deadline.

A remedy for a runoff election scheduled too soon, such as when the date is set by state law that has not yet been brought into compliance with UOCAVA, is to provide for instant runoff ballots. By rank ordering candidates in the first election, voters can show how they would vote in hypothetical runoffs.

### Forty-Five Days Means Forty-Five Days

*United States v. Alabama (Myron H. Thompson, M.D. Ala. 2:12-cv-179; 11th Cir. 14-11298)*

The U.S. Court of Appeals for the Eleventh Circuit determined on February 12, 2015, that Alabama's holding runoff elections forty-two days after primary elections violated UOCAVA as to federal elections, because the timing of the runoff elections did not allow Alabama to send overseas voters their ballots forty-five days in advance of the elections.[38]

---

35. Casarez v. Val Verde County, 967 F. Supp. 917 (W.D. Tex. 1997).

36. Casarez v. Val Verde County, 16 F. Supp. 2d 717 (W.D. Tex. 1998), *aff'd*, 194 F.3d 1308 (5th Cir. 1999) (table).

37. Casarez v. Val Verde County, 27 F. Supp. 2d 749 (W.D. Tex. 1998), *aff'd*, 194 F.3d 1309 (5th Cir. 1999) (table); *see* Damages Payment Receipt, *Casarez*, No. 2:96-cv-108 (W.D. Tex. July 29, 2010), D.E. 177; Order to Satisfy Damages Award, *id.* (June 3, 2010), D.E. 176; Writ of Execution, *id.* (Nov. 16, 2009), D.E. 171.

38. United States v. Alabama, 778 F.3d 926 (11th Cir. 2015).

The Department of Justice filed a federal complaint in the Middle District of Alabama on February 24, 2012, alleging (1) that some of Alabama's counties had sent some overseas absentee ballots out less than forty-five days in advance of the upcoming March 13 primary election and (2) that Alabama's runoff schedule would not allow runoff ballots, if necessary, to be sent out in time.[39] Judge Myron H. Thompson issued a preliminary injunction on March 7 that extended the deadline for casting overseas absentee ballots and required notifications to overseas voters on how ballots could be cast electronically.[40] Judge Thompson rejected the state's arguments that it was not responsible under UOCAVA for ballots sent out late by counties.[41]

Alabama set an election schedule to fill an August 2, 2013, congressional vacancy created by Jo Bonner's resignation with only forty-two days separating a September 24 primary election, a possible November 5 runoff, and a December 17 general election.[42] Judge Thompson ordered Alabama to use instant runoff ballots for the primary election, in which voters rank-order their choices.[43] Judge Thompson also ordered Alabama to offer overseas voters—and provide for express delivery of—tardy runoff ballots reflecting the results of the primary election, which the voters could use to override their primary election rankings[44] Overseas absentee ballots for the general election would include primary election victors as well as candidates in necessary runoffs and allow for party voting.[45]

Judge Thompson granted the government summary judgment in 2014, declaring Alabama's forty-two days between an election and a runoff

---

39. Complaint, United States v. Alabama, No. 2:12-cv-179 (M.D. Ala. Feb. 24, 2012), D.E. 1; United States v. Alabama, 778 F.3d 926, 928, 930–31 (11th Cir. 2015); United States v. Alabama, 998 F. Supp. 2d 1283, 1287 (M.D. Ala. 2014); United States v. Alabama, 857 F. Supp. 2d 1236, 1237–38 (M.D. Ala. 2012).

40. Preliminary Injunction, *United States v. Alabama*, No. 2:12-cv-179 (M.D. Ala. Mar. 7, 2012), D.E. 21; *United States v. Alabama*, 857 F. Supp. 2d 1236.

41. *United States v. Alabama*, 857 F. Supp. 2d at 1238; see *United States v. Alabama*, 998 F. Supp. 2d 1283.

42. Opinion at 1–3, *United States v. Alabama*, No. 2:12-cv-179 (M.D. Ala. July 26, 2013), D.E. 71.

43. *Id.* at 2, 6.

44. *Id.* at 6–7.

45. *Id.* at 7–8.

a violation of UOCAVA for federal elections, a judgment affirmed by the court of appeals.[46]

## Counting Federal Votes on a Ballot That Has Changed for a State Office
*United States v. West Virginia (John T. Copenhaver, Jr., S.D. W. Va. 2:14-cv-27456)*

U.S. District Judge Judge John T. Copenhaver, Jr., Southern District of West Virginia, determined on December 22, 2014, that federal votes on overseas absentee ballots sent out before a candidate change for a state office must be counted.[47]

After absentee ballots were sent to West Virginia overseas voters forty-five days in advance of the November 4, 2014, general election, West Virginia's supreme court of appeals ordered a ballot substitution for a candidate who had withdrawn from the race for district 35 of the state's house of delegates.[48] On November 3, Judge Copenhaver signed a consent decree between West Virginia election officials and the Justice Department extending the deadline for receipt of overseas ballots for federal offices cast by voters registered in district 35 so that the forty-five-day casting period was preserved.[49]

Because the supreme court of appeals' writ of mandamus appeared to nullify district 35 absentee ballots sent out before the candidate substitution, the Justice Department filed a motion on November 6 seeking to have federal votes cast on those ballots counted if the voters did not cast corrected ballots.[50]

---

46. *United States v. Alabama*, 998 F. Supp. 2d 1283, *aff'd*, 778 F.3d 926 (11th Cir. 2015).

47. Opinion Denying a Preliminary Injunction, United States v. West Virginia, No. 2:14-cv-27456 (S.D. W. Va. Dec. 22, 2014), D.E. 22, 2014 WL 7338867.

48. Mandamus Opinion, West Virginia *ex rel.* McDavid v. Tennant, No. 14-939 (W. Va. Oct. 1, 2014), www.courtswv.gov/supreme-court/memo-decisions/fall2014/14-0939memo.pdf, 2014 WL 4922641; Opinion Denying a Preliminary Injunction, *supra* note 47, at 2–3.

49. Consent Decree, *United States v. West Virginia*, No. 2:14-cv-27456 (S.D. W. Va. Nov. 3, 2014), D.E. 5.

50. Motion for Emergency Supplemental Injunctive Relief, *id.* (Nov. 6, 2014), D.E. 6.

Judge Copenhaver denied the Justice Department preliminary relief,[51] but after full briefing he ordered federal votes on the four ballots at issue counted, remedying among other things the voters' uncertainty about the effect of casting two ballots.[52]

## Late Overseas Ballots in Michigan

*United States v. Michigan (Robert J. Jonker, W.D. Mich. 1:12-cv-788)*

Four days in advance of an August 10, 2012, election, U.S. District Judge Robert J. Jonker, Western District of Michigan, approved a stipulated order that, among other things, (1) gave overseas voters extensions beyond election day equal to the number of days late their jurisdictions sent out overseas absentee ballots and (2) permitted Michigan jurisdictions to certify results that could not be affected by outstanding overseas ballots.[53]

One week in advance of Michigan's 2012 federal primary election, the Justice Department filed a federal complaint alleging that "62 [Michigan] cities and townships reported that they failed to send all of their UOCAVA ballots by the June 23, 2012 deadline."[54]

## Allowing for Overseas Voting in a Runoff Election

*United States v. Georgia (Steve C. Jones, N.D. Ga. 1:12-cv-2230; 11th Cir. 13-14065)*

Approximately four weeks in advance of a July 31, 2012, primary election in Georgia, U.S. District Judge Steve C. Jones, Northern District of Georgia, issued an injunction requiring Georgia to extend the deadline for return of absentee ballots and pay for their express delivery should the scheduled August 21 runoff election be necessary, because the runoff election was scheduled for only twenty-one days after the initial primary election.[55]

---

51. Opinion Denying a Preliminary Injunction, *supra* note 47.

52. Opinion, *United States v. West Virginia*, No. 2:14-cv-27456 (S.D. W. Va. Dec. 22, 2014), D.E. 22, 2014 WL 7338867; *see* Notification of Compliance, *id.* (Jan. 22, 2015), D.E. 24.

53. Stipulated Order, United States v. Michigan, No. 1:12-cv-788 (W.D. Mich. Aug. 6, 2012), D.E. 16.

54. Complaint 4, *id.* (July 31, 2012), D.E. 1.

55. United States v. Georgia, 892 F. Supp. 2d 1367, 1378–81 (N.D. Ga. 2012); United States v. Georgia, 952 F. Supp. 2d 1318, 1324 (N.D. Ga. 2013) (summarizing the relief as "extended ballot receipt deadlines, mandatory website content,

Judge Jones issued the immediate relief one court day after a hearing and eight calendar days after the Justice Department filed the complaint.[56] Ruling on summary judgment motions nearly one year later, Judge Jones observed that "Georgia has not passed legislation that provides for a forty-five-day transmittal period for runoff election absentee ballots."[57] Judge Jones ordered Georgia to "submit to the Court written proposed changes to Georgia's election laws that show full compliance with UOCAVA as to all future federal runoff elections."[58]

Rejecting Georgia's proposal for retaining its election calendar but extending the deadline for overseas voting in runoff elections, Judge Jones issued an injunction on July 11, 2013, specifying an election calendar for federal offices that would comply with UOCAVA.[59]

The U.S. Court of Appeals for the Eleventh Circuit dismissed an appeal as moot because 2014 changes to Georgia's election laws brought them into compliance with UOCAVA.[60]

## Judge-Set Primary Election Dates for New York
*United States v. New York (Gary L. Sharpe, N.D.N.Y. 1:10-cv-1214)*

U.S. District Judge Gary L. Sharpe, Northern District of New York, issued an order on January 27, 2012, setting primary election dates in New York for non-presidential primaries until New York enacted a different primary

---

outgoing express ballot transmission, electronic and express ballot return, ballot counting procedures and notice, training of election officials, coordination with the Federal Voting Assistance Program, a press statement, and statistical reporting to the United States").

56. *United States v. Georgia*, 892 F. Supp. 2d at 1369, 1371; Complaint, United States v. Georgia, No. 1:12-cv-2230 (N.D. Ga. June 27, 2012), D.E. 1; Transcript, *id.* (July 3, 2012, filed Aug. 15, 2012), D.E. 17; Minutes, *id.* (July 3, 2012), D.E. 9.

57. *United States v. Georgia*, 952 F. Supp. 2d at 1322.

58. *Id.* at 1333–34.

59. Opinion, *United States v. Georgia*, No. 1:12-cv-2230 (N.D. Ga. July 11, 2013), D.E. 38; *see* order, *id.* (Aug. 21, 2013), D.E. 44 (modifying the election calendar to avoid advance voting during the Memorial Day weekend).

60. United States v. Georgia, 778 F.3d 1201 (11th Cir. 2015); *see* Order, *United States v. Georgia*, No. 1:12-cv-2230 (N.D. Ga. Feb. 27, 2015), D.E. 62 (dismissing the complaint as moot).

election schedule also compliant with UOCAVA.[61] To ensure adequate time between the primary election and the deadline for sending out general election absentee ballots to overseas voters, Judge Sharpe set primary elections for the fourth Tuesday of June.[62]

The Justice Department filed the action to enforce UOCAVA in New York on October 12, 2010.[63] An October 19 consent decree required overseas ballots postmarked or equivalently shown to be cast by the day before the November 2 election to be counted if received by November 24.[64]

Because New York's laws were still not in compliance with UOCAVA as the 2012 election cycle got underway, Judge Sharpe set June 26 as an interim federal primary election date.[65] Later, Judge Sharpe set New York's federal election schedule for 2014[66] and 2016.[67]

## No Need for Court Action If the State Remedies Late Ballots
*Doe v. Miller (Gloria M. Navarro, D. Nev. 2:10-cv-1753)*

In an action brought by a candidate for Nevada's secretary of state, U.S. District Judge Gloria M. Navarro, District of Nevada, denied a remedy for one county's sending out overseas absentee ballots as many as five days late because Nevada had extended the return deadline by six days.[68] The late ballots resulted from a printer's error.[69]

---

61. Opinion, United States v. New York, No. 1:10-cv-1214 (N.D.N.Y. Jan. 27, 2012), D.E. 59 [hereinafter *United States v. New York* Opinion], 2012 WL 254263.

62. *Id.* at 8.

63. Complaint, *id.* (Oct. 12, 2010), D.E. 1.

64. Consent Decree at 7–8, *id.* (Oct. 19, 2010), D.E. 9.

65. *United States v. New York* Opinion, *supra* note 61, at 8; *see* Order, *United States v. New York*, No. 1:10-cv-1214 (N.D.N.Y. Feb. 9, 2012), D.E. 64 (enforcing the court's order in light of "intransigent refusal to comply with a federal mandate").

66. Order, *United States v. New York*, No. 1:10-cv-1214 (N.D.N.Y. Dec. 12, 2013), D.E. 85.

67. Order, *id.* (Oct. 28, 2015), D.E. 87.

68. Opinion, Doe v. Miller, No. 2:10-cv-1753 (D. Nev. Oct. 27, 2010), D.E. 16, 2010 WL 4340804.

69. *Id.* at 3.

The action was filed on October 8, 2010, in advance of the November 2 election, and named as the lead plaintiff an anonymous soldier.[70] Judge Navarro dismissed the action on the papers.[71]

*Thirty-Day Extension for Receipt of Absentee Ballots*
McCain-Palin 2008, Inc. v. Cunningham (Richard L. Williams, E.D. Va. 3:08-cv-709)

U.S. District Judge Richard L. Williams, Eastern District of Virginia, ordered Virginia "to count as validly-cast all timely-requested, but belatedly-mailed absentee ballots that were received within thirty days of the close of polls on November 4, 2008, so long as such ballots are otherwise valid under Virginia law."[72] Judge Williams did not issue this summary judgment until October 15, 2009, however.[73]

The case was filed by John McCain's presidential campaign on November 3, 2008, the day before the election, claiming Virginia's failure to send some overseas voters absentee ballots in time for them to be returned by election day.[74] Judge Williams heard the case at 2:00 p.m. on election day.[75] Judge Williams ordered Virginia to preserve all absentee ballots received after election day.[76]

After the election, on November 17, Judge Williams granted the Justice Department's motion to intervene and dismissed the campaign as a plaintiff.[77] The litigation was brought to a close in 2010 by consent decree.[78]

---

70. Complaint, *id.* (Oct. 8, 2010), D.E. 1.
71. Docket Sheet, *id.* (Oct. 8, 2010).
72. Opinion at 17, United States v. Cunningham, No. 3:08-cv-709 (E.D. Va. Oct. 15, 2009), D.E. 57, 2009 WL 3350028.
73. Docket Sheet, *id.* (Nov. 3, 2008) (D.E. 57, 58).
74. Complaint, *id.* (Nov. 3, 2008), D.E. 1.
75. Minutes, *id.* (Nov. 4, 2008), D.E. 9.
76. Temporary Restraining Order, *id.* (Nov. 4, 2008), D.E. 10; Minutes, *id.* (Nov. 4, 2008), D.E. 9.
77. Order, *id.* (Nov. 17, 2008), D.E. 31.
78. Consent Decree, *id.* (Dec. 14, 2010), D.E. 75.

*Changes to the Ballot After the Sending Out of Absentee Ballots*
United States v. Pennsylvania (1:04-cv-830) and Reitz v. Rendell (1:04-cv-2360)
(Yvette Kane, M.D. Pa.)

Thirteen days in advance of the November 2, 2004, general election, U.S. District Judge Yvette Kane, Middle District of Pennsylvania, denied the government remedies for overseas absentee ballots sent out with Ralph Nader as a candidate for President although Pennsylvania's supreme court had determined on October 19—the previous day—that Nader was not eligible.[79] Votes for Nader would be counted as write-in votes.[80] "UOCAVA voters will, like all other absentee voters in Pennsylvania, vote the ballot that was legally correct at the time they requested and were provided absentee ballots."[81]

The government filed the complaint on April 15, twelve days in advance of the primary election to ensure that late-sent overseas absentee ballots in the primary election would be counted.[82] For the primary election, Judge Kane extended the deadline for receipt of ballots cast before the polls closed from April 23 to May 17.[83]

One week after Judge Kane issued her opinion concerning the general election, parents of two soldiers filed a complaint alleging the soldiers were not sent absentee ballots on time.[84] Two days later, Judge Kane approved a settlement extending the deadline by eight days for receipt of overseas absentee ballots cast before the polls closed.[85]

---

79. Opinion, United States v. Pennsylvania, No. 1:04-cv-830 (M.D. Pa. Oct. 20, 2004), D.E. 33, 2004 WL 2384999.
80. *Id.* at 10.
81. *Id.* at 7.
82. Complaint, *id.* (Apr. 15, 2004), D.E. 1.
83. Preliminary Injunction, *id.* (Apr. 16, 2004), D.E. 7.
84. Complaint, Reitz v. Rendell, No. 1:04-cv-2360 (M.D. Pa. Oct. 27, 2004), D.E. 1.
85. Order, *id.* (Oct. 29, 2004), D.E. 17, 2004 WL 2451454.

## Federal Write-In Absentee Ballot

UOCAVA's section 103 requires the creation of a blank absentee ballot for use in a federal election when an overseas voter has not received the state's absentee ballot in time, despite the voter's requesting it in time.[86]

*Mandatory Acceptance of Federal Write-In Absentee Ballot*
*Bush v. Hillsborough County Canvassing Board (Lacy A. Collier, N.D. Fla. 3:00-cv-533)*

U.S. District Judge Lacey A. Collier, Northern District of Florida, ordered seven Florida counties in the 2000 presidential election to count federal write-in absentee ballots even if the counties had no record of the voters' requesting state absentee ballots.[87]

The complaint was filed by the George W. Bush campaign nineteen days after the 2000 general election, at a time of uncertainty about which presidential candidate had won Florida's electoral votes and therefore the presidency.[88] Judge Collier issued her injunction twelve days later.[89]

Then as now, section 103 provided for use of a federal write-in absentee ballot by overseas voters "who make timely application for, and do not receive, States' absentee ballots."[90] Judge Collier observed that "the federal write-in ballot includes the oath that 'I swear or affirm, under the penalty for perjury, that my application for a regular state absentee ballot was mailed in time....'"[91] Judge Collier concluded, "We must presume, without evidence to the contrary, that if the election official does not have the application on record, it is because of a problem with the overseas mail system or their own clerical error."[92]

---

86. 52 U.S.C. § 20303 (2014).

87. Bush v. Hillsborough Cnty. Canvassing Bd., 123 F. Supp. 2d 1305 (N.D. Fla. 2000).

88. Complaint, Bush v. Hillsborough Cnty. Canvassing Bd., No. 3:00-cv-533 (N.D. Fla. Nov. 26, 2000), D.E. 1.

89. *Bush*, 123 F. Supp. 2d 1305.

90. 52 U.S.C. § 20303(a)(1); Pub. L. No. 99-410, § 103(a), 100 Stat. 924, 925 (1986).

91. *Bush*, 123 F. Supp. 2d at 1317.

92. *Id.*

## Standing

A federal district court held that the rights of UOCAVA voters belong to the voters and not to candidates.

### No Standing for a Candidate's Suit on Behalf of Overseas Voters
*Somers v. All Improperly Filed Candidates (D.S.C. 3:12-cv-1191)*

A three-judge district court, District of South Carolina, held on May 16, 2012, that a candidate did not have standing to pursue the interests of overseas voters in a challenge to election administration following a disqualification of primary election candidates arising from a ruling by the state's supreme court.[93] The candidate was not an overseas voter, she did not show a close relationship with overseas voters, and she did not show that overseas voters lacked access to courts themselves.[94]

The suit followed a May 2 decision by the state's supreme court that candidates commonly violated the text of South Carolina's statutes, which require candidates to "file a statement of economic interests for the preceding calendar year *at the same time and with the same official* with whom the candidate files a declaration of candidacy or petition for nomination."[95] As a result of this decision, many candidates were disqualified from the June 12 primary election.[96] A candidate who was not disqualified filed the federal case on May 4.[97]

As a result of the state court decision, absentee ballots were sent to overseas voters on time for congressional primary elections and absentee ballots were later sent to overseas voters for state primaries once the valid candidates were determined.[98] The candidate's suit alleged that the state court's literal application of state law was a change in voting practices that

---

93. Somers v. S.C. State Election Comm'n, 871 F. Supp. 2d 490 (D.S.C. 2012); *see* Anderson v. S.C. Election Comm'n, 397 S.C. 551, 725 S.E.2d 704 (S.C. 2012).
94. *Somers*, 871 F. Supp. 2d at 497–98.
95. S.C. Code § 8-13-1356(B) (emphasis added).
96. *Somers*, 871 F. Supp. 2d at 493.
97. Complaint, Somers v. All Improperly Filed Candidates, No. 3:12-cv-1191 (D.S.C. May 4, 2012), D.E. 1 [hereinafter *Somers* Complaint]; *Somers*, 871 F. Supp. 2d at 491.
98. *Somers*, 871 F. Supp. 2d at 493–94.

required preclearance pursuant to section 5 of the Voting Rights Act.[99] The candidate argued that sending out federal and state ballots at different times required section 5 preclearance, but voters who could vote in her primary election for the state's senate did not live in a congressional district with a congressional primary for her party.[100]

## Territories

UOCAVA supports an acceptable irony that permits residents of states to retain the right to vote for President and voting members of Congress when residents move to other countries but not when they move to U.S. territories.

UOCAVA nevertheless protects the federal voting rights of territory residents while they are overseas, such as in elections for the territories' nonvoting members of Congress.

### No New York Absentee Voting for New Yorkers Who Move to Puerto Rico

*Romeu v. Cohen (Shira A. Scheindlin, S.D.N.Y. 1:00-cv-2277; 2d Cir. 00-6287 and 00-6303)*

The U.S. Court of Appeals for the Second Circuit held on September 6, 2001, that it was not unconstitutional for New Yorkers who move to another country to retain their rights to vote in New York while New Yorkers

---

99. *Id.* at 491–93 & n.5; *see* Voting Rights Act of 1965, Pub. L. No. 89-110, § 5, 79 Stat. 437, 439, *as amended*, 52 U.S.C. § 10304 (2014) (requiring preclearance of changes to voting procedures in jurisdictions with a certified history of discrimination and requiring that preclearance disputes be heard by a three-judge court).

On June 25, 2013, the Supreme Court declined to hold section 5 unconstitutional, but the Court did hold unconstitutional the criteria for which jurisdictions require section 5 preclearance. Shelby County v. Holder, 570 U.S. ___, 133 S. Ct. 2612 (2013).

100. *Somers*, 871 F. Supp. 2d at 494–97 & n.13.

In a separate action filed on the day before the primary election by disqualified candidates, the same three-judge court held that application of a statute's plain meaning was not a change in election practice requiring section 5 preclearance. Smith v. S.C. Election Comm'n, 874 F. Supp. 2d 483, 495 (D.S.C. 2012).

who move to Puerto Rico lose those rights.[101] "Congress may distinguish between those U.S. citizens formerly residing in a State who live outside the U.S., and those who live in the U.S. territories."[102] In fact, "extend[ing] the vote in federal elections to U.S. citizens formerly citizens of a State now residing in Puerto Rico while not extending it to U.S. citizens residing in Puerto Rico who have never resided in a State . . . would [be] a distinction of questionable fairness."[103]

Xavier Romeu moved from New York to Puerto Rico on May 17, 1999, and he registered to vote in Puerto Rico.[104] Because residents of Puerto Rico cannot vote for President and Vice President, Romeu wanted to vote as an absentee New Yorker in the 2000 presidential election.[105] Knowing that he could not satisfy New York's requirements for absentee voting because he was a resident of another part of the United States, Romeu filed a federal complaint in the Southern District of New York on March 24, 2000.[106] Judge Shira A. Scheindlin permitted Puerto Rico's governor Pedro Rosselló to intervene in support of Romeu's complaint.[107]

Judge Scheindlin ruled that neither UOCAVA nor other impediments to Romeu's voting absentee in New York were unconstitutional.[108]

> While I sympathize with Romeu's plight and applaud his desire to vote in the 2000 Presidential election, I lack the power to provide him any relief. Only a constitutional amendment or Puerto Rican statehood can provide the cure. All I can do is add my voice to those who have urged the appropriate branches of our government to take all necessary steps to ensure that American

---

101. Romeu v. Cohen, 265 F.3d 118 (2d Cir. 2001).

102. *Id.* at 124.

103. *Id.* at 125.

104. *Id.* at 120; Romeu v. Cohen, 121 F. Supp. 2d 264, 267, 269 (S.D.N.Y. 2000).

105. *Romeu*, 121 F. Supp. 2d at 269–70; Pub. L. No. 99-410, 100 Stat. 924 (1986).

106. Docket Sheet, Romeu v. Cohen, No. 1:00-cv-2277 (Mar. 24, 2000) [hereinafter S.D.N.Y. Docket Sheet] (D.E. 1); *Romeu*, 265 F.3d at 122 (2d Cir. 2001); *Romeu*, 121 F. Supp. 2d at 267, 270.

107. *Romeu*, 121 F. Supp. 2d at 268; *Romeu*, 265 F.3d at 122; *see* S.D.N.Y. Docket Sheet, *supra* note 106 (D.E. 16, intervenor's complaint).

108. *Romeu*, 121 F. Supp. 2d 264.

citizens residing in all United States territories be permitted to vote for President and Vice President as soon as possible.[109]

The court of appeals denied the appeals filed by Romeu and Rosselló on October 31.[110] The court of appeals issued its opinion the following September.[111]

## No Votes for President in Puerto Rico

*Igartúa de la Rosa v. United States (Raymond L. Acosta, D.P.R. 3:91-cv-2506; 1st Cir. 94-1174)*

The U.S. Court of Appeals for the First Circuit held in 1994 that UOCAVA does not violate the constitutional rights of Puerto Rico voters by providing for presidential votes by citizens who move from a state to another country while not providing for presidential votes by citizens who move from a state to Puerto Rico.[112]

In 2000, a panel of the court of appeals determined that the 1994 holding controlled and required a reversal of Judge Jaime Pieras, Jr.'s holding that residents of Puerto Rico had a right to vote for President and Vice President.[113]

---

109. *Id.* at 268.

110. *Romeu*, 265 F.3d at 122; *see* Docket Sheet, Romeu v. Cohen, No. 00-6303 (2d Cir. Oct. 10, 2000) (Rosselló's appeal); Docket Sheet, Romeu v. Cohen, No. 00-6287 (2d Cir. Oct. 2, 2000) (Romeu's appeal).

111. *Romeu*, 121 F. Supp. 2d 264.

112. Igartúa de la Rosa v. United States, 32 F.3d 8 (1st Cir.), *aff'g* 842 F. Supp. 607 (D.P.R. 1994); *see* Attorney Gen. of Guam v. United States, 738 F.2d 1017, 1019 (9th Cir. 1984) ("A constitutional amendment would be required to permit [residents of Guam] to vote in a presidential election."); Sanchez v. United States, 376 F. Supp. 239 (D.P.R. 1974) (finding that although "it is inexcusable that there still exists a substantial number of U.S. citizens who cannot legally vote for the President and Vice President of the United States," the ability of Puerto Rico residents to do so would require statehood or a constitutional amendment).

113. Igartúa de la Rosa v. United States, 229 F.3d 80, 84 (1st Cir.), *rev'g* 113 F. Supp. 2d 228 (D.P.R. 2000); *see* Igartúa de la Rosa v. United States, 107 F. Supp. 2d 140, 141 (D.P.R. 2000) ("The present political status of Puerto Rico has enslaved the United States citizens residing in Puerto Rico by preventing them from voting in Presidential and Congressional elections . . . ."); *id.* at 149–50 (concluding that precedent barred a constitutional challenge to UOCAVA).

In a third effort to obtain from the courts presidential voting rights for Puerto Ricans, the court of appeals reaffirmed, in 2005, its earlier holdings en banc.[114]

## No Votes in the District of Columbia for Members of Congress from Maryland

*Howard v. State Administrative Board of Election Laws (J. Frederick Motz, D. Md. 1:96-cv-2558; 4th Cir. 96-2840)*

On November 14, 1996, U.S. District Judge J. Frederick Motz, District of Maryland, held that it was not an unconstitutional deprivation of equal protection to permit Americans living overseas to vote for members of Congress from their last states of residence while denying residents of the District of Columbia a similar voting right.[115]

## Overseas Absentee Ballot Consent Decree in the Virgin Islands

*United States v. Virgin Islands (Curtis V. Gómez, D.V.I. 3:12-cv-69)*

U.S. District Judge Curtis V. Gómez, District of the Virgin Islands, signed a consent decree on September 7, 2012, that specified express mail and email voting options and extended the deadlines for receipt of overseas absentee ballots.[116]

The Justice Department filed a federal complaint in the District of the Virgin Islands on August 31, alleging that for the September 8 primary election for delegate to the U.S. House of Representatives, the Virgin Islands failed to transmit absentee ballots to overseas voters forty-five days in advance of the election, and Virgin Islands election procedures would

---

114. Igartúa-de la Rosa v. United States, 417 F.3d 145 (1st Cir. 2005) (en banc) ("Voting for President and Vice President of the United States is governed neither by rhetoric nor intuitive values but by a provision of the Constitution."), *aff'g* 331 F. Supp. 2d 76 (D.P.R. 2004).

115. Howard v. State Admin. Bd. of Election Laws, 976 F. Supp. 350, 351 (D. Md. 1996), *aff'd*, 122 F.3d 1061 (4th Cir. 1997) (table), *cert. denied*, 522 U.S. 1052 (1998); *see* Docket Sheet, Howard v. State Admin. Bd. of Election Laws, No. 1:96-cv-2558 (Aug. 16, 1996).

116. Consent Decree, United States v. Virgin Islands, No. 3:12-cv-69 (D.V.I. Sept. 7, 2012), D.E. 10.

not result in the timely transmission of general election absentee ballots either.[117]

## Prompt Delivery of Absentee Ballots by Guam
*United States v. Guam (Frances M. Tydingco-Gatewood, D. Guam 1:10-cv-25)*

U.S. District Judge Frances M. Tydingco-Gatewood, District of Guam, enforced UOCAVA in Guam for the November 6, 2010, election of Guam's delegate to the U.S. House of Representatives.[118]

The Justice Department filed a federal complaint in Hagåtña on October 6 to enforce the UOCAVA requirement that absentee ballots be sent to overseas voters at least forty-five days before a federal election.[119]

After an October 13 proceeding,[120] Judge Tydingco-Gatewood (1) ordered compliance with UOCAVA, (2) ordered that cast absentee ballots sent by November 2 and received by November 15 be counted for the congressional delegate race, and (3) ordered Guam to provide the court with reports on its compliance efforts.[121]

For the 2012 elections—a September 1 primary election and the November 6 general election—Guam still had not enacted legislation that was compliant with UOCAVA.[122] Judge Tydingco-Gatewood, therefore, issued a stipulated order requiring Guam to provide UOCAVA voters with email as an electronic option for absentee voting.[123]

---

117. Complaint, *id.* (Aug. 31, 2012), D.E. 1.
118. Order, United States v. Guam, No. 1:10-cv-25 (D. Guam Oct. 13, 2010), D.E. 19.
119. Complaint, *id.* (Oct. 6, 2010), D.E. 1; Motion, *id.* (Oct. 6, 2010), D.E. 2 (seeking a temporary restraining order and a preliminary injunction).
120. Minutes, *id.* (Oct. 13, 2010), D.E. 18.
121. Order, *id.* (Oct. 13, 2010), D.E. 19.
122. Order at 2, *id.* (July 13, 2012), D.E. 27.
123. *Id.* at 2–5; *see* Status Update, *id.* (Aug. 1, 2013), D.E. 30 (confirming Guam's compliance with the order).

# Equal Protection

UOCAVA requires the accommodation of overseas voters. Courts have held that this accommodation cannot include extra days of in-person voting for military and overseas voters without offering other voters the extra in-person days, but the accommodation can include more time for overseas ballots to arrive than for stateside absentee ballots.

## Improperly Providing Additional In-Person Voting Opportunities to Overseas Voters

*Obama for America v. Husted (Peter C. Economus, S.D. Ohio 2:12-cv-636; 6th Cir. 12-4055 and 12-4076)*

On October 5, 2012, the U.S. Court of Appeals for the Sixth Circuit affirmed a district court's preliminary injunction against Ohio's decision to afford overseas voters in-person absentee voting during the three days before election day while denying the same opportunity to local voters.[124]

Three organizations supporting Barack Obama's reelection filed a federal complaint in the Southern District of Ohio on July 17 challenging Ohio's decision to eliminate last-weekend early voting only for voters who did not qualify as military or other overseas voters.[125]

Judge Peter C. Economus granted the plaintiffs a preliminary injunction.[126] Following the court of appeals' affirmance, the Supreme Court denied the defendants a stay of the injunction.[127]

Following summary judgment briefing, Judge Economus granted the plaintiffs a permanent injunction in 2014.[128]

---

124. Obama for Am. v. Husted, 697 F.3d 423 (6th Cir. 2012).

125. Complaint, Obama for Am. v. Husted, No. 2:12-cv-636 (S.D. Ohio July 17, 2012), D.E. 1; *Obama for Am.*, 697 F.3d at 425.

126. Obama for Am. v. Husted, 888 F. Supp. 2d 897 (S.D. Ohio 2012), *aff'd*, 697 F.3d 423; *Obama for Am.*, 697 F.3d at 426.

127. Docket Sheet, Husted v. Obama for Am., No. 12A338 (U.S. Oct. 9, 2012).

128. Opinion, *Obama for Am.*, No. 2:12-cv-636 (S.D. Ohio June 11, 2014), D.E. 89, 2014 WL 2611316.

*Not an Equal Protection Violation to Allow More Time for Receipt of Overseas Absentee Votes Than Stateside Absentee Votes*
Friedman v. Snipes (Alan S. Gold, S.D. Fla. 1:04-cv-22787)

U.S. District Judge Alan S. Gold, Southern District of Florida, held on November 9, 2004, that it was not a violation of equal protection for Florida to require that stateside absentee ballots be received by the time the polls closed while granting an additional ten days for receipt of overseas absentee ballots that are nevertheless cast by election day.[129]

The complaint was filed on election day—November 2—by three voters who were out of town for medical and education reasons and who did not receive their absentee ballots until the day before the election at the earliest.[130] On November 3, Judge Gold issued a temporary restraining order pending additional hearing that defendant counties segregate stateside absentee votes received after the deadline for stateside votes but before the deadline for overseas votes.[131]

# Privacy

In a democracy, many election records are necessarily public, but certain voting records must be safeguarded as private, the secret ballot a principal example.[132]

UOCAVA expressly requires privacy "[t]o the extent practicable" for overseas absentee ballot applications[133] and transmissions.[134]

---

129. Friedman v. Snipes, 345 F. Supp. 2d 1356, 1370–82 (S.D. Fla. 2004).

130. *Id.* at 1361–63; Complaint, Friedman v. Snipes, No. 1:04-cv-22787 (S.D. Fla. Nov. 2, 2004), D.E. 1; *see* Amended Complaint, *id.* (Nov. 4, 2004), D.E. 18.

131. Order, *Friedman*, No. 1:04-cv-22787 (S.D. Fla. Nov. 3, 2004), D.E. 15; *Friedman*, 345 F. Supp. 2d at 1358 & n.1.

132. *See* 52 U.S.C. § 20301(b)(9)(B) (2014) (including the secret ballot among the responsibilities of the chief federal UOCAVA enforcement officer).

133. *Id.* § 20302(e)(6)(B).

134. *Id.* § 20302(f)(3)(B).

## Privacy Protections Apply to Requesting Voter Registration Applications, Not to Submitting Them

*Project Vote/Voting for America, Inc. v. Long (Rebecca Beach Smith, E.D. Va. 2:10-cv-75; 4th Cir. 11-1809)*

Affirming a district court judgment that the National Voter Registration Act (NVRA) requires election authorities to provide records of voter registration applications, in a lawsuit involving concerns that college students' registration applications were improperly denied, the U.S. Court of Appeals for the Fourth Circuit determined on June 15, 2012, that the MOVE Act's privacy provisions were not in conflict with the district court's ruling.[135]

Concerned that voter registrations were improperly rejected for students at the historically African-American Norfolk State University in advance of the 2008 general election, Project Vote filed a federal complaint in the Eastern District of Virginia on February 16, 2010, to enforce its request for completed Norfolk voter registration applications.[136] Granting Project Vote summary judgment in 2011, U.S. District Judge Rebecca Beach Smith held that privacy concerns did not relieve Norfolk election authorities from their obligation under the NVRA to provide Project Vote with the requested records.[137]

"Disclosure of the completed voter registration applications does not implicate the MOVE Act's security and privacy protections, which only apply to 'the voter registration and absentee ballot *application request process*,' 42 U.S.C. § 1973ff-1(e)(6) (emphasis added), and absentee ballots. *Id.* § 1973ff-1(f)(3)."[138]

---

135. Project Vote/Voting for Am., Inc. v. Long, 682 F.3d 331, 339 (4th Cir. 2012).

136. Complaint, Project Vote/Voting for Am., Inc. v. Long, No. 2:10-cv-75 (E.D. Va. Feb. 16, 2010), D.E. 1.

137. Project Vote/Voting for Am., Inc. v. Long, 813 F. Supp. 2d 738 (E.D. Va. 2011); *see* 52 U.S.C. 20507 (2014); Robert Timothy Reagan, Motor Voter: The National Voter Registration Act 38 (Federal Judicial Center 2014); *see also* Project Vote/Voting for Am., Inc., 752 F. Supp. 2d 697 (E.D. Va. 2010) (denying a motion to dismiss the case); Project Vote/Voting for Am., Inc., 275 F.R.D. 473 (E.D. Va. 2011) (staying judgment pending appeal).

138. *Project Vote/Voting for Am., Inc.*, 813 F. Supp. 2d at 743 (citing previous codifications of 52 U.S.C. § 20302(e)(6) and (f)(3)).

The court of appeals agreed that the MOVE Act's "privacy provisions protect information transmitted during the process of *requesting*—not submitting—a registration application."[139]

## State Elections

In 2010, a federal district judge held that even in state elections overseas voters have a federal constitutional right to vote that cannot be abridged by unreasonable absentee balloting delays.

### Overseas Voters' Fundamental Right to Vote

Doe v. Walker (Roger W. Titus, D. Md. 8:10-cv-2646)

U.S. District Judge Roger W. Titus, District of Maryland, held on October 29, 2010, that Maryland's due date for overseas absentee ballots in elections for state offices deprived overseas voters of their fundamental right to vote, so Judge Titus extended the deadline for receipt of cast ballots for the November 2 election from November 12 to November 22.[140]

A military voters' rights group filed the complaint on behalf of itself and an anonymous military officer—who used a pseudonym to protect his military mission—on September 23, forty days in advance of the election.[141] Maryland met the UOCAVA deadline of September 18 for federal

---

139. *Project Vote/Voting for Am., Inc.*, 682 F.3d at 338–39.

On August 22, 2012, Judge Smith awarded $184,880.25 in fees and costs to the plaintiff. Project Vote/Voting for Am., Inc., 887 F. Supp. 2d 704 (E.D. Va. 2012). A January 30, 2013, consent decree resolved redaction issues. Consent Decree, *Project Vote/Voting for Am., Inc.*, No. 2:10-cv-75 (E.D. Va. Jan. 30, 2013), D.E. 114; *see* Order, Project Vote/Voting for Am., Inc., No. 12-2142 (4th Cir. Jan. 31, 2013), D.E. 32 (dismissing a redaction appeal as settled, also applying to No. 12-2146); Project Vote/Voting for Am., Inc., 889 F. Supp. 2d 778 (E.D. Va. 2012) (denying the defendants' request for certain redactions).

140. Doe v. Walker, 746 F. Supp. 2d 667 (D. Md. 2010).

141. Complaint, Doe v. Walker, No. 8:10-cv-2646 (D. Md. Sept. 23, 2010), D.E. 1; *Doe*, 746 F. Supp. 2d at 672.

offices by sending overseas voters federal absentee ballots on time and absentee ballots including state offices beginning on October 8, following the September 27 certification of state-office primary election results.[142]

Judge Titus observed that Maryland's November 12 deadline for receipt of overseas absentee ballots allowed for at most thirty-five days.[143] Because some ballots did not go out until October 9, the Saturday of a holiday weekend, mailing might not have been effective until Tuesday, which was only thirty-one days before cast ballots were due.[144]

## Conclusion

Protection of the elective franchise for citizens in military service has expanded to include citizens living abroad. For federal elections, absentee ballots must be available for delivery at least forty-five days in advance of the election. Courts will often be asked to craft or approve remedies until state and local election laws and practices come into compliance with the federal Uniformed and Overseas Citizens Absentee Voting Act.

---

142. *Doe*, 746 F. Supp. 2d at 672 (noting that the federal absentee ballot would only be counted if the voter did not cast a state absentee ballot with both state and federal offices included).

143. *Id.* at 677.

144. *Id.*; *see id.* ("The Department of Defense states that the Army's wartime standard for first class mail delivery is 12 to 18 days from its point of origin in the United States to the individual service member.").

# Appendix: The Uniformed and Overseas Citizens Absentee Voting Act (52 U.S.C. §§ 20301 to 20311)[145]

[Section 101:] § 20301. Federal responsibilities[146]

*(a) Presidential designee*

The President shall designate the head of an executive department to have primary responsibility for Federal functions under this subchapter.

*(b) Duties of Presidential designee*

The Presidential designee shall—

(1) consult State and local election officials in carrying out this subchapter, and ensure that such officials are aware of the requirements of this Act;

(2) prescribe an official post card form, containing both an absentee voter registration application and an absentee ballot application, for use by the States as required under section 20302(a)(4) of this title [UOCAVA section 102(a)(4)];

(3) carry out section 20303 of this title [UOCAVA section 103] with respect to the Federal write-in absentee ballot for absent uniformed services voters and overseas voters in general elections for Federal office;

(4) prescribe a suggested design for absentee ballot mailing envelopes;

(5) compile and distribute (A) descriptive material on State absentee registration and voting procedures, and (B) to the extent practicable, facts relating to specific elections, including dates, offices involved, and the text of ballot questions;

(6) not later than the end of each year after a Presidential election year, transmit to the President and the Congress a report on the effectiveness of assistance under this subchapter, including a statistical analysis of uniformed services voter participation, a separate statistical analysis of overseas nonmilitary participation, and a description of State-Federal cooperation;

(7) prescribe a standard oath for use with any document under this subchapter affirming that a material misstatement of fact in the completion of such a document may constitute grounds for a conviction for perjury;

---

145. Pub. L. No. 99-410, 100 Stat. 924 (1986), *as amended* (42 U.S.C. §§ 1973ff to 1973ff-7 until September 2014).

146. Formerly 42 U.S.C. § 1973ff.

(8) carry out section 20304 of this title [UOCAVA section 103A] with respect to the collection and delivery of marked absentee ballots of absent overseas uniformed services voters in elections for Federal office;

(9) to the greatest extent practicable, take such actions as may be necessary—

    (A) to ensure that absent uniformed services voters who cast absentee ballots at locations or facilities under the jurisdiction of the Presidential designee are able to do so in a private and independent manner; and

    (B) to protect the privacy of the contents of absentee ballots cast by absentee uniformed services voters and overseas voters while such ballots are in the possession or control of the Presidential designee;

(10) carry out section 20305 of this title [UOCAVA section 103B] with respect to Federal Voting Assistance Program Improvements; and

(11) working with the Election Assistance Commission and the chief State election official of each State, develop standards—

    (A) for States to report data on the number of absentee ballots transmitted and received under section 20302(c) of this title [UOCAVA section 102(c)] and such other data as the Presidential designee determines appropriate; and

    (B) for the Presidential designee to store the data reported.

## *(c) Duties of other Federal officials*

### *(1) In general*

The head of each Government department, agency, or other entity shall, upon request of the Presidential designee, distribute balloting materials and otherwise cooperate in carrying out this subchapter.

### *(2) Administrator of General Services*

As directed by the Presidential designee, the Administrator of General Services shall furnish official post card forms (prescribed under subsection (b) of this section) and Federal write-in absentee ballots (prescribed under section 20303 of this title [UOCAVA section 103]).

## *(d) Authorization of appropriations for carrying out Federal Voting Assistance Program Improvements*

There are authorized to be appropriated to the Presidential designee such sums as are necessary for purposes of carrying out subsection (b)(10).

[Section 102:] § 20302. State responsibilities[147]

*(a) In general*

Each State shall—
> (1) permit absent uniformed services voters and overseas voters to use absentee registration procedures and to vote by absentee ballot in general, special, primary, and runoff elections for Federal office;
>
> (2) accept and process, with respect to any election for Federal office, any otherwise valid voter registration application and absentee ballot application from an absent uniformed services voter or overseas voter, if the application is received by the appropriate State election official not less than 30 days before the election;
>
> (3) permit absent uniformed services voters and overseas voters to use Federal write-in absentee ballots (in accordance with section 20303 of this title [UOCAVA section 103]) in general elections for Federal office;
>
> (4) use the official post card form (prescribed under section 20301 of this title [UOCAVA section 101]) for simultaneous voter registration application and absentee ballot application;
>
> (5) if the State requires an oath or affirmation to accompany any document under this subchapter, use the standard oath prescribed by the Presidential designee under section 20301(b)(7) of this title [UOCAVA section 101(b)(7)];
>
> (6) in addition to any other method of registering to vote or applying for an absentee ballot in the State, establish procedures—
>> (A) for absent uniformed services voters and overseas voters to request by mail and electronically voter registration applications and absentee ballot applications with respect to general, special, primary, and runoff elections for Federal office in accordance with subsection (e);
>>
>> (B) for States to send by mail and electronically (in accordance with the preferred method of transmission designated by the absent uniformed services voter or overseas voter under subparagraph (C)) voter registration applications and absentee ballot applications requested under subparagraph (A) in accordance with subsection (e); and
>>
>> (C) by which the absent uniformed services voter or overseas voter can designate whether the voter prefers that such voter registration application or absentee ballot application be transmitted by mail or electronically;

---

147. Formerly 42 U.S.C. § 1973ff-1.

(7) in addition to any other method of transmitting blank absentee ballots in the State, establish procedures for transmitting by mail and electronically blank absentee ballots to absent uniformed services voters and overseas voters with respect to general, special, primary, and runoff elections for Federal office in accordance with subsection (f);

(8) transmit a validly requested absentee ballot to an absent uniformed services voter or overseas voter—

    (A) except as provided in subsection (g), in the case in which the request is received at least 45 days before an election for Federal office, not later than 45 days before the election; and

    (B) in the case in which the request is received less than 45 days before an election for Federal office—

        (i) in accordance with State law; and

        (ii) if practicable and as determined appropriate by the State, in a manner that expedites the transmission of such absentee ballot;

(9) if the State declares or otherwise holds a runoff election for Federal office, establish a written plan that provides absentee ballots are made available to absent uniformed services voters and overseas voters in manner* that gives them sufficient time to vote in the runoff election;

(10) carry out section 20304(b)(1) of this title [UOCAVA section 103A(b)(1)] with respect to the processing and acceptance of marked absentee ballots of absent overseas uniformed services voters; and

(11) report data on the number of absentee ballots transmitted and received under subsection (c) and such other data as the Presidential designee determines appropriate in accordance with the standards developed by the Presidential designee under section 20301(b)(11) of this title [UOCAVA section 101(b)(11)].

## (b) Designation of single State office to provide information on registration and absentee ballot procedures for all voters in State

### (1) In general

Each State shall designate a single office which shall be responsible for providing information regarding voter registration procedures and absentee ballot procedures to be used by absent uniformed services voters and overseas voters with respect to elections for Federal office (including procedures relating to the use of the Federal write-in absentee ballot) to all absent uniformed services voters and overseas voters who wish to register to vote or vote in any jurisdiction in the State.

---

* So in original. Probably should be "in a manner."

*(2) Recommendation regarding use of office to accept and process materials*

Congress recommends that the State office designated under paragraph (1) be responsible for carrying out the State's duties under this Act, including accepting valid voter registration applications, absentee ballot applications, and absentee ballots (including Federal write-in absentee ballots) from all absent uniformed services voters and overseas voters who wish to register to vote or vote in any jurisdiction in the State.

*(c) Report on number of absentee ballots transmitted and received*

Not later than 90 days after the date of each regularly scheduled general election for Federal office, each State and unit of local government which administered the election shall (through the State, in the case of a unit of local government) submit a report to the Election Assistance Commission (established under the Help America Vote Act of 2002 [42 U.S.C. 15301 et seq.]) on the combined number of absentee ballots transmitted to absent uniformed services voters and overseas voters for the election and the combined number of such ballots which were returned by such voters and cast in the election, and shall make such report available to the general public.

*(d) Registration notification*

With respect to each absent uniformed services voter and each overseas voter who submits a voter registration application or an absentee ballot request, if the State rejects the application or request, the State shall provide the voter with the reasons for the rejection.

*(e) Designation of means of electronic communication for absent uniformed services voters and overseas voters to request and for States to send voter registration applications and absentee ballot applications, and for other purposes related to voting information*

*(1) In general*

Each State shall, in addition to the designation of a single State office under subsection (b), designate not less than 1 means of electronic communication—

(A) for use by absent uniformed services voters and overseas voters who wish to register to vote or vote in any jurisdiction in the State to request voter registration applications and absentee ballot applications under subsection (a)(6);

(B) for use by States to send voter registration applications and absentee ballot applications requested under such subsection; and

(C) for the purpose of providing related voting, balloting, and election information to absent uniformed services voters and overseas voters.

*(2) Clarification regarding provision of multiple means of electronic communication*

A State may, in addition to the means of electronic communication so designated, provide multiple means of electronic communication to absent uniformed services voters and overseas voters, including a means of electronic communication for the appropriate jurisdiction of the State.

*(3) Inclusion of designated means of electronic communication with informational and instructional materials that accompany balloting materials*

Each State shall include a means of electronic communication so designated with all informational and instructional materials that accompany balloting materials sent by the State to absent uniformed services voters and overseas voters.

*(4) Availability and maintenance of online repository of State contact information*

The Federal Voting Assistance Program of the Department of Defense shall maintain and make available to the public an online repository of State contact information with respect to elections for Federal office, including the single State office designated under subsection (b) and the means of electronic communication designated under paragraph (1), to be used by absent uniformed services voters and overseas voters as a resource to send voter registration applications and absentee ballot applications to the appropriate jurisdiction in the State.

*(5) Transmission if no preference indicated*

In the case where an absent uniformed services voter or overseas voter does not designate a preference under subsection (a)(6)(C), the State shall transmit the voter registration application or absentee ballot application by any delivery method allowable in accordance with applicable State law, or if there is no applicable State law, by mail.

### (6) Security and privacy protections

#### (A) Security protections

To the extent practicable, States shall ensure that the procedures established under subsection (a)(6) protect the security and integrity of the voter registration and absentee ballot application request processes.

#### (B) Privacy protections

To the extent practicable, the procedures established under subsection (a)(6) shall ensure that the privacy of the identity and other personal data of an absent uniformed services voter or overseas voter who requests or is sent a voter registration application or absentee ballot application under such subsection is protected throughout the process of making such request or being sent such application.

## (f) Transmission of blank absentee ballots by mail and electronically

### (1) In general

Each State shall establish procedures—

    (A) to transmit blank absentee ballots by mail and electronically (in accordance with the preferred method of transmission designated by the absent uniformed services voter or overseas voter under subparagraph (B)) to absent uniformed services voters and overseas voters for an election for Federal office; and

    (B) by which the absent uniformed services voter or overseas voter can designate whether the voter prefers that such blank absentee ballot be transmitted by mail or electronically.

### (2) Transmission if no preference indicated

In the case where an absent uniformed services voter or overseas voter does not designate a preference under paragraph (1)(B), the State shall transmit the ballot by any delivery method allowable in accordance with applicable State law, or if there is no applicable State law, by mail.

### (3) Security and privacy protections

#### (A) Security protections

To the extent practicable, States shall ensure that the procedures established under subsection (a)(7) protect the security and integrity of absentee ballots.

*(B) Privacy protections*

To the extent practicable, the procedures established under subsection (a)(7) shall ensure that the privacy of the identity and other personal data of an absent uniformed services voter or overseas voter to whom a blank absentee ballot is transmitted under such subsection is protected throughout the process of such transmission.

*(g) Hardship exemption*

*(1) In general*

If the chief State election official determines that the State is unable to meet the requirement under subsection (a)(8)(A) with respect to an election for Federal office due to an undue hardship described in paragraph (2)(B), the chief State election official shall request that the Presidential designee grant a waiver to the State of the application of such subsection. Such request shall include—

(A) a recognition that the purpose of such subsection is to allow absent uniformed services voters and overseas voters enough time to vote in an election for Federal office;

(B) an explanation of the hardship that indicates why the State is unable to transmit absent uniformed services voters and overseas voters an absentee ballot in accordance with such subsection;

(C) the number of days prior to the election for Federal office that the State requires absentee ballots be transmitted to absent uniformed services voters and overseas voters; and

(D) a comprehensive plan to ensure that absent uniformed services voters and overseas voters are able to receive absentee ballots which they have requested and submit marked absentee ballots to the appropriate State election official in time to have that ballot counted in the election for Federal office, which includes—

(i) the steps the State will undertake to ensure that absent uniformed services voters and overseas voters have time to receive, mark, and submit their ballots in time to have those ballots counted in the election;

(ii) why the plan provides absent uniformed services voters and overseas voters sufficient time to vote as a substitute for the requirements under such subsection; and

(iii) the underlying factual information which explains how the plan provides such sufficient time to vote as a substitute for such requirements.

*(2) Approval of waiver request*

After consulting with the Attorney General, the Presidential designee shall approve a waiver request under paragraph (1) if the Presidential designee determines each of the following requirements are met:

(A) The comprehensive plan under subparagraph (D) of such paragraph provides absent uniformed services voters and overseas voters sufficient time to receive absentee ballots they have requested and submit marked absentee ballots to the appropriate State election official in time to have that ballot counted in the election for Federal office.

(B) One or more of the following issues creates an undue hardship for the State:

(i) The State's primary election date prohibits the State from complying with subsection (a)(8)(A).

(ii) The State has suffered a delay in generating ballots due to a legal contest.

(iii) The State Constitution prohibits the State from complying with such subsection.

*(3) Timing of waiver*

*(A) In general*

Except as provided under subparagraph (B), a State that requests a waiver under paragraph (1) shall submit to the Presidential designee the written waiver request not later than 90 days before the election for Federal office with respect to which the request is submitted. The Presidential designee shall approve or deny the waiver request not later than 65 days before such election.

*(B) Exception*

If a State requests a waiver under paragraph (1) as the result of an undue hardship described in paragraph (2)(B)(ii), the State shall submit to the Presidential designee the written waiver request as soon as practicable. The Presidential designee shall approve or deny the waiver request not later than 5 business days after the date on which the request is received.

*(4) Application of waiver*

A waiver approved under paragraph (2) shall only apply with respect to the election for Federal office for which the request was submitted. For each subsequent election for Federal office, the Presidential designee shall only approve a waiver if the State has submitted a request under paragraph (1) with respect to such election.

*(h) Tracking marked ballots*

The chief State election official, in coordination with local election jurisdictions, shall develop a free access system by which an absent uniformed services voter or overseas voter may determine whether the absentee ballot of the absent uniformed services voter or overseas voter has been received by the appropriate State election official.

*(i) Prohibiting refusal to accept applications for failure to meet certain requirements*

A State shall not refuse to accept and process any otherwise valid voter registration application or absentee ballot application (including the official post card form prescribed under section 20301 of this title [UOCAVA section 101]) or marked absentee ballot submitted in any manner by an absent uniformed services voter or overseas voter solely on the basis of the following:

    (1) Notarization requirements.
    (2) Restrictions on paper type, including weight and size.
    (3) Restrictions on envelope type, including weight and size.

[Section 103:] § 20303. Federal write-in absentee ballot in general elections for Federal office for absent uniformed services voters and overseas voters[148]

*(a) In general*

  *(1) Federal write-in absentee ballot*

The Presidential designee shall prescribe a Federal write-in absentee ballot (including a secrecy envelope and mailing envelope for such ballot) for use in general, special, primary, and runoff elections for Federal office by absent uniformed services voters and overseas voters who make timely application for, and do not receive, States,[*] absentee ballots.

  *(2) Promotion and expansion of use of Federal write-in absentee ballots*

    *(A) In general*

Not later than December 31, 2011, the Presidential designee shall adopt procedures to promote and expand the use of the Federal write-in absentee ballot as a back-up measure to vote in elections for Federal office.

---

148. Formerly 42 U.S.C. § 1973ff-2.
\* So in original. Probably should be "States'."

*(B) Use of technology*

Under such procedures, the Presidential designee shall utilize technology to implement a system under which the absent uniformed services voter or overseas voter may—

(i) enter the address of the voter or other information relevant in the appropriate jurisdiction of the State, and the system will generate a list of all candidates in the election for Federal office in that jurisdiction; and

(ii) submit the marked Federal write-in absentee ballot by printing the ballot (including complete instructions for submitting the marked Federal write-in absentee ballot to the appropriate State election official and the mailing address of the single State office designated under section 20302(b) of this title [UOCAVA section 102(b)]).

*(C) Authorization of appropriations*

There are authorized to be appropriated to the Presidential designee such sums as may be necessary to carry out this paragraph.

*(b) Submission and processing*

Except as otherwise provided in this subchapter, a Federal write-in absentee ballot shall be submitted and processed in the manner provided by law for absentee ballots in the State involved. A Federal write-in absentee ballot of an absent uniformed services voter or overseas voter shall not be counted—

(1) in the case of a ballot submitted by an overseas voter who is not an absent uniformed services voter, if the ballot is submitted from any location in the United States;

(2) if the application of the absent uniformed services voter or overseas voter for a State absentee ballot is received by the appropriate State election official after the later of—

(A) the deadline of the State for receipt of such application; or

(B) the date that is 30 days before the general election; or

(3) if a State absentee ballot of the absent uniformed services voter or overseas voter is received by the appropriate State election official not later than the deadline for receipt of the State absentee ballot under State law.

*(c) Special rules*

The following rules shall apply with respect to Federal write-in absentee ballots:

(1) In completing the ballot, the absent uniformed services voter or overseas voter may designate a candidate by writing in the name of the candidate

or by writing in the name of a political party (in which case the ballot shall be counted for the candidate of that political party).

(2) In the case of the offices of President and Vice President, a vote for a named candidate or a vote by writing in the name of a political party shall be counted as a vote for the electors supporting the candidate involved.

(3) Any abbreviation, misspelling, or other minor variation in the form of the name of a candidate or a political party shall be disregarded in determining the validity of the ballot, if the intention of the voter can be ascertained.

*(d) Second ballot submission; instruction to absent uniformed services voter or overseas voter*

An absent uniformed services voter or overseas voter who submits a Federal write-in absentee ballot and later receives a State absentee ballot, may submit the State absentee ballot. The Presidential designee shall assure that the instructions for each Federal write-in absentee ballot clearly state that an absent uniformed services voter or overseas voter who submits a Federal write-in absentee ballot and later receives and submits a State absentee ballot should make every reasonable effort to inform the appropriate State election official that the voter has submitted more than one ballot.

*(e) Use of approved State absentee ballot in place of Federal write-in absentee ballot*

The Federal write-in absentee ballot shall not be valid for use in a general, special, primary, or runoff election for Federal office if the State involved provides a State absentee ballot that—

(1) at the request of the State, is approved by the Presidential designee for use in place of the Federal write-in absentee ballot; and

(2) is made available to absent uniformed services voters and overseas voters at least 60 days before the deadline for receipt of the State ballot under State law.

*(f) Prohibiting refusal to accept ballot for failure to meet certain requirements*

A State shall not refuse to accept and process any otherwise valid Federal write-in absentee ballot submitted in any manner by an absent uniformed services voter or overseas voter solely on the basis of the following:

(1) Notarization requirements.

(2) Restrictions on paper type, including weight and size.

(3) Restrictions on envelope type, including weight and size.

*(g) Certain States exempted*

A State is not required to permit use of the Federal write-in absentee ballot, if, on and after August 28, 1986, the State has in effect a law providing that—

    (1) a State absentee ballot is required to be available to any voter described in section 20310(5)(A) of this title [UOCAVA section 107(5)(A)] at least 90 days before the general, special, primary, or runoff election for Federal office involved; and

    (2) a State absentee ballot is required to be available to any voter described in section 20310(5)(B) or (C) of this title [UOCAVA section 107(5)(B) or (C)], as soon as the official list of candidates in the general, special, primary, or runoff election for Federal office is complete.

## [Section 103A:] § 20304. Procedures for collection and delivery of marked absentee ballots of absent overseas uniformed services voters[149]

*(a) Establishment of procedures*

The Presidential designee shall establish procedures for collecting marked absentee ballots of absent overseas uniformed services voters in regularly scheduled general elections for Federal office, including absentee ballots prepared by States and the Federal write-in absentee ballot prescribed under section 20303 of this title [UOCAVA section 103], and for delivering such marked absentee ballots to the appropriate election officials.

*(b) Delivery to appropriate election officials*

    *(1) In general*

Under the procedures established under this section, the Presidential designee shall implement procedures that facilitate the delivery of marked absentee ballots of absent overseas uniformed services voters for regularly scheduled general elections for Federal office to the appropriate election officials, in accordance with this section, not later than the date by which an absentee ballot must be received in order to be counted in the election.

    *(2) Cooperation and coordination with the United States Postal Service*

The Presidential designee shall carry out this section in cooperation and coordination with the United States Postal Service, and shall provide expedited mail delivery service for all such marked absentee ballots of absent uniformed services voters that are collected on or before the deadline described in paragraph (3) and then transferred to the United States Postal Service.

---

149. Formerly 42 U.S.C. § 1973ff-2a.

*(3) Deadline described*

*(A) In general*

Except as provided in subparagraph (B), the deadline described in this paragraph is noon (in the location in which the ballot is collected) on the seventh day preceding the date of the regularly scheduled general election for Federal office.

*(B) Authority to establish alternative deadline for certain locations*

If the Presidential designee determines that the deadline described in subparagraph (A) is not sufficient to ensure timely delivery of the ballot under paragraph (1) with respect to a particular location because of remoteness or other factors, the Presidential designee may establish as an alternative deadline for that location the latest date occurring prior to the deadline described in subparagraph (A) which is sufficient to provide timely delivery of the ballot under paragraph (1).

*(4) No postage requirement*

In accordance with section 3406 of title 39, such marked absentee ballots and other balloting materials shall be carried free of postage.

*(5) Date of mailing*

Such marked absentee ballots shall be postmarked with a record of the date on which the ballot is mailed.

*(c) Outreach for absent overseas uniformed services voters on procedures*

The Presidential designee shall take appropriate actions to inform individuals who are anticipated to be absent overseas uniformed services voters in a regularly scheduled general election for Federal office to which this section applies of the procedures for the collection and delivery of marked absentee ballots established pursuant to this section, including the manner in which such voters may utilize such procedures for the submittal of marked absentee ballots pursuant to this section.

*(d) Absent overseas uniformed services voter defined*

In this section, the term "absent overseas uniformed services voter" means an overseas voter described in section 20310(5)(A) of this title [UOCAVA section 107(5)(A)].

*(e) Authorization of appropriations*

There are authorized to be appropriated to the Presidential designee such sums as may be necessary to carry out this section.

[Section 103B:] § 20305. Federal Voting Assistance Program Improvements[150]

*(a) Duties*

The Presidential designee shall carry out the following duties:
    (1) Develop online portals of information to inform absent uniformed services voters regarding voter registration procedures and absentee ballot procedures to be used by such voters with respect to elections for Federal office.
    (2) Establish a program to notify absent uniformed services voters of voter registration information and resources, the availability of the Federal postcard application, and the availability of the Federal write-in absentee ballot on the military Global Network, and shall use the military Global Network to notify absent uniformed services voters of the foregoing 90, 60, and 30 days prior to each election for Federal office.

*(b) Clarification regarding other duties and obligations*

Nothing in this section shall relieve the Presidential designee of their duties and obligations under any directives or regulations issued by the Department of Defense, including the Department of Defense Directive 1000.04 (or any successor directive or regulation) that is not inconsistent or contradictory to the provisions of this section.

*(c) Authorization of appropriations*

There are authorized to be appropriated to the Federal Voting Assistance Program of the Department of Defense (or a successor program) such sums as are necessary for purposes of carrying out this section.

[Section 104:] § 20306. Prohibition of refusal of applications on grounds of early submission[151]

A State may not refuse to accept or process, with respect to any election for Federal office, any otherwise valid voter registration application or absentee ballot application (including the postcard form prescribed under section 20301 of this title

---

    150. Formerly 42 U.S.C. § 1973ff-2b.
    151. Formerly 42 U.S.C. § 1973ff-3.

[UOCAVA section 101]) submitted by an absent uniformed services voter during a year on the grounds that the voter submitted the application before the first date on which the State otherwise accepts or processes such applications for that year submitted by absentee voters who are not members of the uniformed services.

[Section 105:] § 20307. Enforcement[152]

*(a) In general*

The Attorney General may bring a civil action in an appropriate district court for such declaratory or injunctive relief as may be necessary to carry out this subchapter.

*(b) Report to Congress*

Not later than December 31 of each year, the Attorney General shall submit to Congress an annual report on any civil action brought under subsection (a) during the preceding year.

[Section 105A:] § 20308. Reporting requirements[153]

*(a) Report on status of implementation and assessment of programs*

Not later than 180 days after October 28, 2009, the Presidential designee shall submit to the relevant committees of Congress a report containing the following information:

(1) The status of the implementation of the procedures established for the collection and delivery of marked absentee ballots of absent overseas uniformed services voters under section 20304 of this title [UOCAVA section 103A], and a detailed description of the specific steps taken towards such implementation for the regularly scheduled general election for Federal office held in November 2010.

(2) An assessment of the effectiveness of the Voting Assistance Officer Program of the Department of Defense, which shall include the following:

(A) A thorough and complete assessment of whether the Program, as configured and implemented as of October 28, 2009, is effectively assisting absent uniformed services voters in exercising their right to vote.

(B) An inventory and explanation of any areas of voter assistance in which the Program has failed to accomplish its stated objectives and effectively assist absent uniformed services voters in exercising their right to vote.

---

152. Formerly 42 U.S.C. § 1973ff-4.
153. Formerly 42 U.S.C. § 1973ff-4a.

(C) As necessary, a detailed plan for the implementation of any new program to replace or supplement voter assistance activities required to be performed under this Act.

(3) A detailed description of the specific steps taken towards the implementation of voter registration assistance for absent uniformed services voters under section 1566a of title 10.

*(b) Annual report on effectiveness of activities and utilization of certain procedures*

Not later than March 31 of each year, the Presidential designee shall transmit to the President and to the relevant committees of Congress a report containing the following information:

(1) An assessment of the effectiveness of activities carried out under section 20305 of this title [UOCAVA section 103B], including the activities and actions of the Federal Voting Assistance Program of the Department of Defense, a separate assessment of voter registration and participation by absent uniformed services voters, a separate assessment of voter registration and participation by overseas voters who are not members of the uniformed services, and a description of the cooperation between States and the Federal Government in carrying out such section.

(2) A description of the utilization of voter registration assistance under section 1566a of title 10, which shall include the following:

(A) A description of the specific programs implemented by each military department of the Armed Forces pursuant to such section.

(B) The number of absent uniformed services voters who utilized voter registration assistance provided under such section.

(3) In the case of a report submitted under this subsection in the year following a year in which a regularly scheduled general election for Federal office is held, a description of the utilization of the procedures for the collection and delivery of marked absentee ballots established pursuant to section 20304 of this title [UOCAVA section 103A], which shall include the number of marked absentee ballots collected and delivered under such procedures and the number of such ballots which were not delivered by the time of the closing of the polls on the date of the election (and the reasons such ballots were not so delivered).

*(c) Definitions*

In this section:

*(1) Absent overseas uniformed services voter*

The term "absent overseas uniformed services voter" has the meaning given such term in section 20304(d) of this title [UOCAVA section 103A(d)].

*(2) Presidential designee*

The term "Presidential designee" means the Presidential designee under section 20301(a) of this title [UOCAVA section 101(a)].

*(3) Relevant committees of Congress defined*

The term "relevant committees of Congress" means—
    (A) the Committees on Appropriations, Armed Services, and Rules and Administration of the Senate; and
    (B) the Committees on Appropriations, Armed Services, and House Administration of the House of Representatives.

[Section 106:] § 20309. Effect on certain other laws[154]

The exercise of any right under this subchapter shall not affect, for purposes of any Federal, State, or local tax, the residence or domicile of a person exercising such right.

[Section 107:] § 20310. Definitions[155]

As used in this subchapter, the term—
    (1) "absent uniformed services voter" means—
        (A) a member of a uniformed service on active duty who, by reason of such active duty, is absent from the place of residence where the member is otherwise qualified to vote;
        (B) a member of the merchant marine who, by reason of service in the merchant marine, is absent from the place of residence where the member is otherwise qualified to vote; and
        (C) a spouse or dependent of a member referred to in subparagraph (A) or (B) who, by reason of the active duty or service of the member, is absent from the place of residence where the spouse or dependent is otherwise qualified to vote;

---

154. Formerly 42 U.S.C. § 1973ff-5.
155. Formerly 42 U.S.C. § 1973ff-6.

(2) "balloting materials" means official post card forms (prescribed under section 20301 of this title [UOCAVA section 101]), Federal write-in absentee ballots (prescribed under section 20303 of this title [UOCAVA section 103]), and any State balloting materials that, as determined by the Presidential designee, are essential to the carrying out of this subchapter;

(3) "Federal office" means the office of President or Vice President, or of Senator or Representative in, or Delegate or Resident Commissioner to, the Congress;

(4) "member of the merchant marine" means an individual (other than a member of a uniformed service or an individual employed, enrolled, or maintained on the Great Lakes or the inland waterways)—

(A) employed as an officer or crew member of a vessel documented under the laws of the United States, or a vessel owned by the United States, or a vessel of foreign-flag registry under charter to or control of the United States; or

(B) enrolled with the United States for employment or training for employment, or maintained by the United States for emergency relief service, as an officer or crew member of any such vessel;

(5) "overseas voter" means—

(A) an absent uniformed services voter who, by reason of active duty or service is absent from the United States on the date of the election involved;

(B) a person who resides outside the United States and is qualified to vote in the last place in which the person was domiciled before leaving the United States; or

(C) a person who resides outside the United States and (but for such residence) would be qualified to vote in the last place in which the person was domiciled before leaving the United States.

(6) "State" means a State of the United States, the District of Columbia, the Commonwealth of Puerto Rico, Guam, the Virgin Islands, and American Samoa;

(7) "uniformed services" means the Army, Navy, Air Force, Marine Corps, and Coast Guard, the commissioned corps of the Public Health Service, and the commissioned corps of the National Oceanic and Atmospheric Administration; and

(8) "United States", where used in the territorial sense, means the several States, the District of Columbia, the Commonwealth of Puerto Rico, Guam, the Virgin Islands, and American Samoa.

## § 20311. Technology pilot program[156]

*(a) Definitions*

In this section:

*(1) Absent uniformed services voter*

The term "absent uniformed services voter" has the meaning given such term in section 107(1) of the Uniformed and Overseas Citizens Absentee Voting Act (42 U.S.C. 1973ff–6(1)).

*(2) Overseas voter*

The term "overseas voter" has the meaning given such term in section 107(5) of such Act [42 U.S.C. 1973ff–6(5)].

*(3) Presidential designee*

The term "Presidential designee" means the individual designated under section 101(a) of such Act [42 U.S.C. 1973ff(a)].

*(b) Establishment*

*(1) In general*

The Presidential designee may establish 1 or more pilot programs under which the feasibility of new election technology is tested for the benefit of absent uniformed services voters and overseas voters claiming rights under the Uniformed and Overseas Citizens Absentee Voting Act (42 U.S.C. 1973ff et seq.).

*(2) Design and conduct*

The design and conduct of a pilot program established under this subsection—
>  (A) shall be at the discretion of the Presidential designee; and
>  (B) shall not conflict with or substitute for existing laws, regulations, or procedures with respect to the participation of absent uniformed services voters and military voters in elections for Federal office.

*(c) Considerations*

In conducting a pilot program established under subsection (b), the Presidential designee may consider the following issues:

---

156. Formerly 42 U.S.C. § 1973ff-7.

(1) The transmission of electronic voting material across military networks.

(2) Virtual private networks, cryptographic voting systems, centrally controlled voting stations, and other information security techniques.

(3) The transmission of ballot representations and scanned pictures in a secure manner.

(4) Capturing, retaining, and comparing electronic and physical ballot representations.

(5) Utilization of voting stations at military bases.

(6) Document delivery and upload systems.

(7) The functional effectiveness of the application or adoption of the pilot program to operational environments, taking into account environmental and logistical obstacles and State procedures.

*(d) Reports*

The Presidential designee shall submit to Congress reports on the progress and outcomes of any pilot program conducted under this subsection, together with recommendations—

(1) for the conduct of additional pilot programs under this section; and

(2) for such legislation and administrative action as the Presidential designee determines appropriate.

*(e) Technical assistance*

*(1) In general*

The Election Assistance Commission and the National Institute of Standards and Technology shall provide the Presidential designee with best practices or standards in accordance with electronic absentee voting guidelines established under the first sentence of section 1604(a)(2) of the National Defense Authorization Act for Fiscal Year 2002 (Public Law 107–107; 115 Stat. 1277; 42 U.S.C. 1973ff note), as amended by section 567 of the Ronald W. Reagan National Defense Authorization Act for Fiscal Year 2005 (Public Law 108–375; 118 Stat. 1919) to support the pilot program or programs.

*(2) Report*

In the case in which the Election Assistance Commission has not established electronic absentee voting guidelines under such section 1604(a)(2), as so amended, by not later than 180 days after October 28, 2009, the Election Assistance Commission shall submit to the relevant committees of Congress a report containing the following information:

(A) The reasons such guidelines have not been established as of such date.

(B) A detailed timeline for the establishment of such guidelines.
(C) A detailed explanation of the Commission's actions in establishing such guidelines since October 28, 2004.

## *(3) Relevant committees of Congress defined*

In this subsection, the term "relevant committees of Congress" means—
(A) the Committees on Appropriations, Armed Services, and Rules and Administration of the Senate; and
(B) the Committees on Appropriations, Armed Services, and House Administration of the House of Representatives.

## *(f) Authorization of appropriations*

There are authorized to be appropriated such sums as are necessary to carry out this section.

# The Federal Judicial Center

**Board**
The Chief Justice of the United States, *Chair*
Judge Curtis L. Collier, U.S. District Court for the Eastern District of Tennessee
Magistrate Judge Jonathan W. Feldman, U.S. District Court for the Western District of New York
Judge Kent A. Jordan, U.S. Court of Appeals for the Third Circuit
Judge Kimberly J. Mueller, U.S. District Court for the Eastern District of California
Chief Judge C. Ray Mullins, U.S. Bankruptcy Court for the Northern District of Georgia
Judge George Z. Singal, U.S. District Court for the District of Maine
Judge David S. Tatel, U.S. Court of Appeals for the District of Columbia Circuit
James C. Duff, Director of the Administrative Office of the U.S. Courts

**Director**
Judge Jeremy D. Fogel

**Deputy Director**
John S. Cooke

**About the Federal Judicial Center**
The Federal Judicial Center is the research and education agency of the federal judicial system. It was established by Congress in 1967 (28 U.S.C. §§ 620–629), on the recommendation of the Judicial Conference of the United States.

By statute, the Chief Justice of the United States chairs the Center's Board, which also includes the director of the Administrative Office of the U.S. Courts and seven judges elected by the Judicial Conference.

The organization of the Center reflects its primary statutory mandates. The Education Division plans and produces education and training for judges and court staff, including in-person programs, video programs, publications, curriculum packages for in-court training, and Web-based programs and resources. The Research Division examines and evaluates current and alternative federal court practices and policies. This research assists Judicial Conference committees, who request most Center research, in developing policy recommendations. The Center's research also contributes substantially to its educational mission. The Federal Judicial History Office helps courts and others study and preserve federal judicial history. The International Judicial Relations Office provides information to judicial and legal officials from foreign countries and assesses how to inform federal judicial personnel of developments in international law and other court systems that may affect their work. Two units of the Director's Office—the Information Technology Office and the Editorial & Information Services Office—support Center missions through technology, editorial and design assistance, and organization and dissemination of Center resources.

www.ingramcontent.com/pod-product-compliance
Lightning Source LLC
Chambersburg PA
CBHW061224180526
45170CB00003B/1155